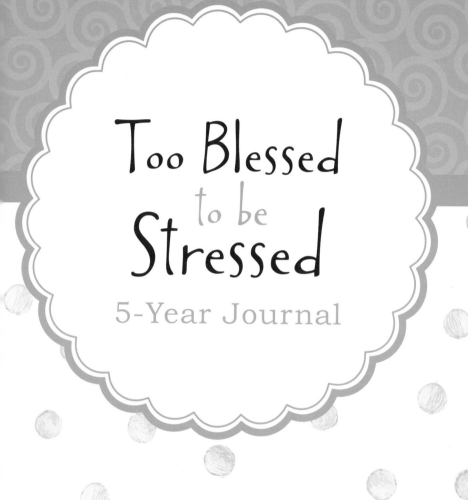

Too Blessed to be Stressed

5-Year Journal

Inspiration and Encouragement from
Debora M. Coty

BARBOUR BOOKS
An Imprint of Barbour Publishing, Inc.

January 1

Take a deep breath. Close your eyes. Exhale slowly. There.
You've just taken the first step in stress reduction.

January 2

Good judgment comes from bad experiences
and a lot of that comes from bad judgment.
UNKNOWN

January 3

YEAR

YEAR

YEAR

YEAR

YEAR

Time to LOL!

I knew it was time to address my stress issues when my growl grew louder
than the dog's, and my fam tactfully suggested I get a rabies shot.

January 4

YEAR

YEAR

YEAR

YEAR

YEAR

God will never let you down.
1 CORINTHIANS 10:13 MSG

January 5

YEAR

YEAR

YEAR

YEAR

YEAR

Pressure creates both diamonds and volcanoes.

January 6

YEAR

YEAR

YEAR

YEAR

YEAR

Let a few things go. Tomorrow, release a few more. In time those tasks will quit nagging at you, and you'll literally feel the stress rocks in your stomach disintegrate into dust!

January 7

YEAR

YEAR

YEAR

YEAR

YEAR

When we live life in a hurry,
we end up weary. . .in a hurry.
KERI WYATT KENT

January 8

The LORD said, "I will go with you and give you peace."
EXODUS 33:14 CEV

January 9

YEAR

YEAR

YEAR

YEAR

YEAR

Give up perfectionism.
Ain't nobody perfect but Jesus, and you're not Him.

January 10

....
....
....
....
....

....
....
....
....

....
....
....
....

....
....
....
....

....
....
....
....

Half our life is spent trying to find something to do
with the time we have rushed through life trying to save.
WILL ROGERS

January 11

When you're tempted to forsake your devotional moments, family time, or prayer walks to toothbrush the grout, disinfect the toilets, or scrub the baseboards like Martha on steroids, remember Jesus' words to His beloved spiritual sister: *"Martha, dear Martha, you're fussing far too much and getting yourself all worked up over nothing"* (John 10:41 MSG).

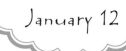

January 12

YEAR

....
....
....
....
....

YEAR

....
....
....
....
....

YEAR

....
....
....
....
....

YEAR

....
....
....
....
....

YEAR

....
....
....
....
....

The joy of the LORD is your strength.
NEHEMIAH 8:10 NIV

January 13

YEAR

YEAR

YEAR

YEAR

YEAR

Positive self-talk is a *huge* part of everyday stress management.
By choosing an upbeat attitude, our outlook becomes much more
optimistic and consequently much less stress-producing.

January 14

Tweak your tone! "Impossible" is a brick wall compared
to "this may take some work." Wouldn't you rather tackle a
project that's "challenging," rather than "unmanageable"?

January 15

YEAR

YEAR

YEAR

YEAR

YEAR

Unless you're the reigning world champion, there will always be someone better than you at a specific skill. So what? You don't need another tiara.

January 16

Let all things be done decently and in order.
1 CORINTHIANS 14:40 KJV

January 17

YEAR

YEAR

YEAR

YEAR

YEAR

Rearrange the following priorities in order of importance to you:
"me" time, family, faith, work, achieving success, appearance,
relationships, schedules. On which three do you spend the most time?

January 18

YEAR

YEAR

YEAR

YEAR

YEAR

Act positive to actually become positive. . . . In other words,
putting on a happy-face mask truly makes us feel happier!

January 19

Memorize Philippians 4:13. Repeat frequently. Trust God and act on it! *I can do everything through Christ, who gives me strength.*
PHILIPPIANS 4:13 NLT

January 20

YEAR

....
....
....
....
....

YEAR

....
....
....
....
....

YEAR

....
....
....
....
....

YEAR

....
....
....
....
....

YEAR

....
....
....
....

When we allow negative self-talk, we're not only limiting ourselves,
we're limiting our God. . .the Creator of the Universe. . .the One
who is ready to fill us with expectancy, hope, and potential.

January 21

YEAR

YEAR

YEAR

YEAR

YEAR

Words are powerful.
They have the ability to change our perception
of our own abilities from limited to limitless.

January 22

Whether you think you can or think you can't—you are right.

HENRY FORD

January 23

YEAR

YEAR

YEAR

YEAR

YEAR

Recycle glass, paper, cardboard, plastics, aluminum, and smiles.
The latter lasts forever.

January 24

YEAR

YEAR

YEAR

YEAR

YEAR

If our minds are ruled by our desires, we will die.
But if our minds are ruled by the Spirit, we will have life and peace.
ROMANS 8:6 CEV

January 25

YEAR

YEAR

YEAR

YEAR

YEAR

Keep your eyes on Jesus. . . . Remember, it's His power,
His presence that ultimately heals. God really
does do broken-heart surgery.

January 26

YEAR

YEAR

YEAR

YEAR

YEAR

The next time you feel like yelling, "Stick a toothpick in me; I'm done!"
remember that although our "oven" days are difficult—often painful—
those are the times we grow and mature in our faith.

January 27

Be your own BFF! Speak to yourself like you would your very best friend.
Make it a point to be encouraging, uplifting, affirming,
light, and humorous (you'll listen better!).

January 28

YEAR

....

....

....

....

YEAR

....

....

....

....

YEAR

....

....

....

....

YEAR

....

....

....

....

YEAR

....

....

....

....

*[Jesus said,] "Martha, dear Martha, you're fussing far
too much and getting yourself worked up over nothing."*
LUKE 10:41 MSG

January 29

YEAR

YEAR

YEAR

YEAR

YEAR

Do everything in moderation, including moderation.
BEN FRANKLIN

January 30

YEAR

YEAR

YEAR

YEAR

Beauty is always there; we just don't see it
when our eyes are focused on our to-do lists.

January 31

YEAR

YEAR

YEAR

YEAR

YEAR

Papa God wants to give us His peace.

February 1

YEAR

YEAR

YEAR

YEAR

YEAR

*Fix your thoughts on what is true, and honorable, and right,
and pure, and lovely, and admirable. Think about things
that are excellent and worthy of praise.*
PHILIPPIANS 4:8 NLT

February 2

YEAR

YEAR

YEAR

YEAR

YEAR

Time to LOL!
Housekeeping is a perpetual lesson in futility.
Cleaning an occupied house is like combing your hair in a hurricane.

February 3

Circumstances don't have to control us. We can't change every situation,
but through the Lord's power we can choose our response to them.
And that makes the difference between victory and defeat.

February 4

YEAR

YEAR

YEAR

YEAR

YEAR

Communicate with Papa God every day in every way.
Pray as if your life depends on it—because it does!

February 5

Whatever you do in word or deed,
do all in the name of the Lord.
COLOSSIANS 3:17 NASB

February 6

Grasp every opportunity to recognize God's
fingerprints in the details of your everyday life.

February 7

YEAR

YEAR

YEAR

YEAR

YEAR

There's never enough time to do all the nothing you want.
BILL WATTERSON, *CALVIN AND HOBBES*

February 8

Healing is a dollar-off coupon, not a blow-out sale. It's an incremental process. Step by tiny step, just keep moving in the right direction and eventually you'll get there. You will!

February 9

YEAR

YEAR

YEAR

YEAR

YEAR

Yes, my soul, find rest in God;
my hope comes from him.
PSALM 62:5 NIV

February 10

YEAR

YEAR

YEAR

YEAR

YEAR

Think about a recent time when you faced devastating,
unexpected loss. How did you deal with it? Have you come
to the conclusion that you're too blessed to be stressed?

February 11

YEAR

YEAR

YEAR

YEAR

YEAR

How can we turn off the fret faucet? When the mental obsession recorder hits REPLAY for the tenth time, lay your problems at the foot of the cross. Jesus will take them off your hands.

February 12

YEAR

YEAR

YEAR

YEAR

YEAR

Time to LOL!
Distraction is your friend. . . . Positive input reduces negative output.
You can't bite your nails while scrubbing the linoleum.

February 13

YEAR

YEAR

YEAR

YEAR

YEAR

Generations come and generations go,
but the earth remains forever.
ECCLESIASTES 1:4 NIV

February 14

The joy of the Lord brings splashes of
color into our black and white world.

February 15

YEAR

YEAR

YEAR

YEAR

YEAR

"Be anxious for nothing" takes on new meaning when you grasp the fact that anxiety does absolutely nothing for you.

February 16

YEAR

[ ]

YEAR

[ ]

YEAR

[ ]

YEAR

[ ]

YEAR

[ ]

Every evening I turn my worries over to God.
He's going to be up all night anyway.
MARY C. CROWLEY

February 17

YEAR

....

....

....

....

....

YEAR

....

....

....

....

....

YEAR

....

....

....

....

....

YEAR

....

....

....

....

....

YEAR

....

....

....

....

....

*He has never let you down, never looked the other way when
you were being kicked around. He has never wandered off
to do his own thing; he has been right there, listening.*
PSALM 22:24 MSG

February 18

No matter how organized you are, something will eventually
go awry. Don't freak. Expect it. Take control of your
attitude so that your attitude doesn't take control of you.

February 19

True strength lies in submission, which permits one to dedicate
his life, through devotion, to something beyond himself.
HENRY MILLER

February 20

YEAR

YEAR

YEAR

YEAR

YEAR

Today, read Psalm 4 (it's short).
How, like David, can we find peace in our distress?

February 21

YEAR

YEAR

YEAR

YEAR

YEAR

*"Come to me, all you who are weary
and burdened, and I will give you rest."*
MATTHEW 11:28 NIV

February 22

YEAR

YEAR

YEAR

YEAR

YEAR

There's hope for us, sisters! You and I can be Cinderella!
Through Papa God's power working within us,
we can transform into a new, improved version of
ourselves beyond our most extravagant imaginings.

February 23

YEAR

YEAR

YEAR

YEAR

YEAR

The sun hasn't disappeared just because it's temporarily obscured by clouds. Sometimes those silver linings are just a belly laugh away.

February 24

YEAR

YEAR

YEAR

YEAR

YEAR

What makes you laugh? A roly-poly puppy? Funny movies?
A favorite comedian? So when was the last time
you set yourself up for a good belly laugh?

February 25

YEAR

YEAR

YEAR

YEAR

YEAR

Everyone born of God overcomes the world.
1 JOHN 5:4 NIV

February 26

YEAR

YEAR

YEAR

YEAR

YEAR

Time to LOL!
Nature abhors a vacuum. And so do I.
ANNE GIBBONS

February 27

YEAR

YEAR

YEAR

YEAR

YEAR

Humor is God's weapon against worry, anxiety, and fear. It's a powerful
salve for the skinned knees of the spirit. . .healing, revitalizing, protecting
us against toxic infections like bitterness, defeat, or depression.

February 28

YEAR

YEAR

YEAR

YEAR

YEAR

God meets us wherever we are. . . . Wherever we need Him to
bail us out of the stress-pool, He's already there with His bucket.

March 1

YEAR
....
....
....
....
....
....

YEAR
....
....
....
....
....
....

YEAR
....
....
....
....
....
....

YEAR
....
....
....
....
....
....

YEAR
....
....
....
....
....
....

Our purpose is to please God, not people.
1 THESSALONIANS 2:4 NLT

March 2

YEAR

YEAR

YEAR

YEAR

YEAR

There is no peace in striving with your own
strength to hold on to what you may lose.
RUBYE GOODLETT

March 3

YEAR

YEAR

YEAR

YEAR

YEAR

March 4

YEAR

YEAR

YEAR

YEAR

YEAR

Time to LOL!
Consciousness is simply that annoying time between naps.

March 5

YEAR
....

YEAR
....

YEAR
....

YEAR
....

YEAR
....

*Do nothing from selfishness or empty conceit, but with humility
of mind regard one another as more important than yourselves.*
PHILIPPIANS 2:3 NASB

March 6

When you're totally dependent on God's grace,
He never lets you down.

March 7

YEAR

YEAR

YEAR

YEAR

Lord, please chill my internal inferno and help me not to have an "ity" day. You know, an *uppity* day in which I demonstrate, in no particular order, *density, banality, crudity, calamity, stupidity, disunity, ferocity, futility, audacity,* and especially *insanity.* Thank You for Your gracious generosity. Amen.

March 8

YEAR

YEAR

YEAR

YEAR

YEAR

Time to LOL!
My soul's had enough chicken soup, thank you. Now it needs a little
stimulation; you know—a choc-tastic attitude adjustment, mocha
milkshake for the mind, chinning up with chocolate chunks. . .

March 9

"Who of you by worrying can add a single hour to your life? Since you cannot do this very little thing, why do you worry about the rest?"
LUKE 12:25–26 NIV

March 10

YEAR

YEAR

YEAR

YEAR

Time to LOL!

My newest political agenda is to petition Congress to legislate a daily American siesta. We could close down all businesses from 1 to 3 p.m., curl up on little mats like kindergartners (after mandatory cookies and milk, of course), catch some zzz's and become a kinder, gentler nation because of it.

March 11

Happy naps are little slices of heaven that revive our energy,
clarity, and motivation; our front line of defense against
temperament-raging fatigue, which results in acute nastiness.

March 12

Those who loved you and were helped by you will remember you when forget-me-nots have withered. Carve your name on hearts, not marble.

CHARLES SPURGEON

March 13

YEAR

YEAR

YEAR

YEAR

YEAR

For God is not a God of disorder, but of peace.
1 Corinthians 14:33 NIV

March 14

YEAR

YEAR

YEAR

YEAR

YEAR

God is not our afflict*or*; no, He's the helper of the afflict*ed*.
That's you and me. He's not the enemy; He's on our team.

March 15

YEAR

....

....

....

....

....

YEAR

....

....

....

....

....

YEAR

....

....

....

....

....

YEAR

....

....

....

....

....

YEAR

....

....

....

....

....

When you feel wounded, where do you turn for healing?

March 16

YEAR

YEAR

YEAR

YEAR

YEAR

Stress management professionals recommend that you engage
in one activity weekly just for fun. But, hey, why stop at one?

March 17

YEAR

YEAR

YEAR

YEAR

YEAR

I will still be the same when you are old and gray,
and I will take care of you.
ISAIAH 46:4 CEV

March 18

YEAR

YEAR

YEAR

YEAR

YEAR

Drag your thoughts away from your troubles. . .by the ears,
by the heels, or any other way you can manage it.
MARK TWAIN

March 19

Jesus Himself stole away for a rest break
and encouraged His buds to do likewise.

March 20

We are treasured. Cherished. Adored. Papa God wants nothing more than to cuddle with us, crooning His comfort and peace into our troubled hearts. Anytime. Anywhere.

March 21

YEAR

YEAR

YEAR

YEAR

YEAR

If we are "out of our mind," as some say, it is for God.
2 CORINTHIANS 5:13 NIV

March 22

YEAR

YEAR

YEAR

YEAR

YEAR

We may not be able to eliminate stress from our crazy lives, but we can empower ourselves to weather the stress better by pursuing rejuvenating activities that refill our joy tanks rather than suck us bone dry.

March 23

YEAR

YEAR

YEAR

YEAR

YEAR

Time to LOL!
No woman is an island (but she can dream!).

March 24

Mercy is completely undeserved; I think that's what makes it so
exquisitely valuable. Take a moment and treasure the free gift
of God's mercy in giving His Son as payment for your sins.

March 25

YEAR

YEAR

YEAR

YEAR

YEAR

*When you have eaten and are satisfied, praise the
LORD your God for the good land he has given you.*
DEUTERONOMY 8:10 NIV

March 26

YEAR

YEAR

YEAR

YEAR

YEAR

Behave outwardly like Christ, pray for His power, and your inner emotions and thoughts will gradually transform to become more Christlike. Fake it at first if you have to—the *act* becomes *fact* as God changes you from the outside in.

March 27

YEAR

....
....
....
....
....
....

YEAR

....
....
....
....
....
....

YEAR

....
....
....
....
....
....

YEAR

....
....
....
....
....
....

YEAR

....
....
....
....
....

Our heavenly Father takes pleasure in being our own personal EMS:
Everyday Miracle Service.

March 28

YEAR

YEAR

YEAR

YEAR

YEAR

You don't love someone for their looks or their clothes or for
their fancy car, but because they sing a song only you can hear.
UNKNOWN

March 29

YEAR

YEAR

YEAR

YEAR

YEAR

*"First clean the inside of the cup and dish,
and then the outside also will be clean."*
MATTHEW 23:26 NIV

March 30

YEAR

YEAR

YEAR

YEAR

YEAR

Like scum building up in the corners of the shower,
emotional residue can dirty the edges of our peace without us
even realizing it. As unsettling as it can be at the moment,
it's important to deal with situations as they arise and not carry
them around for weeks or even years like stinky loaded diapers.

March 31

YEAR

....

....

....

....

....

....

YEAR

....

....

....

....

....

....

YEAR

....

....

....

....

....

....

YEAR

....

....

....

....

....

....

YEAR

....

....

....

....

....

....

Some say Christians should be sober and serious and silent
as the grave, but I say Jesus came *out* of the grave and
that's the best reason in the world to celebrate!

April 1

There's absolutely nothing you're tempted to worry about
that you won't be better off talking to God about instead.
GREG LAURIE

April 2

Don't waste your time on useless work,
mere busywork, the barren pursuits of darkness.
EPHESIANS 5:16 MSG

April 3

YEAR

YEAR

YEAR

YEAR

YEAR

Time to LOL!
A socially acceptable way to release frustration: organized sports.
(Better than beating up your trash can or shredding your panty hose.)

April 4

YEAR

YEAR

YEAR

YEAR

YEAR

Girlfriends fill the holes in our relationships with others. . .especially the sinkholes. Girlfriends make us laugh when we least expect it.

April 5

YEAR

YEAR

YEAR

YEAR

YEAR

Papa God didn't intend for our bodies to stay in the same positions hour after hour or to perform the same functions repeatedly without resting. Paced, daily timeouts for a few simple stretching exercises can bring immense relief to painful necks and tight shoulders.

April 6

YEAR

YEAR

YEAR

YEAR

YEAR

Pride lands you flat on your face;
humility prepares you for honors.
PROVERBS 29:23 MSG

April 7

YEAR

YEAR

YEAR

YEAR

YEAR

Time to LOL!
Age is something that doesn't matter, unless you are a cheese.
BILLIE BURKE, AKA GLINDA THE GOOD WITCH IN *THE WIZARD OF OZ*

April 8

Trust is the cornerstone to acquiring peace. We can relax in complete
security, knowing our Creator is looking out for our best interests.
Relax. Uncoil. Chill. Let go of the steering wheel.

April 9

YEAR

YEAR

YEAR

YEAR

YEAR

Marinating in faith produces the choicest priority cuts.

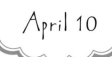

April 10

YEAR

....

....

....

....

....

YEAR

....

....

....

....

....

YEAR

....

....

....

....

....

YEAR

....

....

....

....

....

YEAR

....

....

....

....

....

When you lie down, your sleep will be sweet.
PROVERBS 3:24 NIV

April 11

YEAR

YEAR

YEAR

YEAR

YEAR

Time to LOL!
Life's made up of little accomplishments—
don't obsess over the holes and miss the doughnuts!

April 12

YEAR

YEAR

YEAR

YEAR

YEAR

We must keep our arsenals full of ammo by memorizing verses
and studying our Bibles so our flaming arrows are lit and ready
to shoot the moment we're jumped by the enemy, the devil.

April 13

YEAR

YEAR

YEAR

YEAR

YEAR

Today, read Isaiah 46:4 (NLT): *I will be your God throughout your lifetime—until your hair is white with age. I made you, and I will care for you. I will carry you along and save you.* How does God's reassurance that He'll take care of you when you have snow on your roof affect the way you live today?

April 14

YEAR

YEAR

YEAR

YEAR

YEAR

I know everything you have done, and you are not cold or hot.
I wish you were either one or the other.
REVELATION 3:15 CEV

April 15

YEAR

YEAR

YEAR

YEAR

YEAR

Time to LOL!
Set aside half an hour every day to do all your worrying,
then take a nap during this period.
UNKNOWN

April 16

YEAR

....
....
....
....
....

YEAR

....
....
....
....
....

YEAR

....
....
....
....
....

YEAR

....
....
....
....
....

YEAR

....
....
....
....

How do you replenish your faith reserves on a daily basis?

April 17

YEAR

....

....

....

....

....

YEAR

....

....

....

....

....

YEAR

....

....

....

....

....

YEAR

....

....

....

....

....

YEAR

....

....

....

....

We can't help the flat feet and connect-the-dot freckles our
children inherit, but we *can* intentionally transfer specific
character-molding traits. . . . It's never too late to lay the
foundation for a strong and lasting faith dynasty!

April 18

YEAR

YEAR

YEAR

YEAR

YEAR

When my life was slipping away, I remembered you—
and in your holy temple you heard my prayer.
JONAH 2:7 CEV

April 19

YEAR

YEAR

YEAR

YEAR

YEAR

There are perks to a lifestyle of gratitude. After all,
I can't be depressed and thankful at the same time.

April 20

YEAR

YEAR

YEAR

YEAR

YEAR

We go through turbulent seasons, but we have to remember that the storms won't last forever. Dawn always breaks after a long, dark night.

April 21

YEAR

YEAR

YEAR

YEAR

YEAR

Pour out your feelings to Papa God. He understands loss—His beloved Son was ruthlessly beaten and killed. Go ahead, pound on His chest. Scream. Sob. He's a very big God. He can take it.

April 22

The righteous eat to their hearts' content,
but the stomach of the wicked goes hungry.
PROVERBS 13:25 NIV

April 23

YEAR

YEAR

YEAR

YEAR

For fast-acting relief, try slowing down.
LILY TOMLIN

April 24

God's specialty, His forte, His marvelous operational technique
is to use inadequate, frightened people to serve as His
hands and feet. Yahweh's courage is more than enough.

April 25

Mother Teresa, prayer warrior tiny in stature but enormous in spirit, once said, "God speaks in the silence of the heart. Listening is the beginning of prayer."

April 26

Happiness makes you smile;
sorrow can crush you.
PROVERBS 15:13 CEV

April 27

YEAR

YEAR

YEAR

YEAR

YEAR

God is the Lord of details, you know.
And He loves to surprise us.

April 28

YEAR

....
....
....
....
....

YEAR

....
....
....
....
....

YEAR

....
....
....
....
....

YEAR

....
....
....
....
....

YEAR

....
....
....
....

Doesn't it knock boulders of stress from our weary,
sagging shoulders to realize that God's sovereignty,
His ultimate authority over this universe He created, takes
precedence over the tiny pebbles of control we thought we had?

April 29

YEAR

YEAR

YEAR

YEAR

YEAR

The Holy Spirit is ready and willing to meet us, greet us, fill us, and fulfill us at the drop of a paper dental bib. . .or in a carpool line. . .or a McDonald's drive-through. He will be there smiling.

April 30

YEAR
....
....
....
....
....

YEAR
....
....
....
....
....

YEAR
....
....
....
....
....

YEAR
....
....
....
....
....

YEAR
....
....
....
....
....

*I've decided that there's nothing better to do than go ahead
and have a good time and get the most we can out of life.*
ECCLESIASTES 3:12 MSG

May 1

YEAR

YEAR

YEAR

YEAR

YEAR

Healing takes effort on our part; we can't just sit like a limp, wounded lump and wait for it to hit us. We have to dig deep for the courage to reach out for help from the very source of our pain. Or so we perceive. But then by God's grace we will find what was really never lost.

May 2

Eternal life is the dessert on the smorgasbord of faith.

May 3

YEAR

YEAR

YEAR

YEAR

YEAR

All peace isn't created equal. The world's peace is based on the absence of conflict; God's peace comes in the midst of conflict.

May 4

YEAR

YEAR

YEAR

YEAR

YEAR

A cord of three strands is not quickly torn apart.
ECCLESIASTES 4:12 NASB

May 5

YEAR

YEAR

YEAR

YEAR

YEAR

Papa God's rejuvenating touch of joy creates the ultimate face-lift!

May 6

YEAR

YEAR

YEAR

YEAR

YEAR

Trust in our heavenly Father is meant to literally become part of us.
A lifestyle. An underlying belief system that is woven into the fabric
of our being as much as the color of our eyes. Not something we
have to remember to apply. . .like sunscreen or lipstick.

May 7

YEAR

YEAR

YEAR

YEAR

YEAR

We can either bless people or blast them with our tongues. . .
like little lethal cannons. I choose to be a blesser. How about you?

May 8

YEAR

YEAR

YEAR

YEAR

YEAR

*But He gives a greater grace. . . . "God is opposed
to the proud, but gives grace to the humble."*
JAMES 4:6 NASB

May 9

YEAR

YEAR

YEAR

YEAR

YEAR

Time to LOL!
I used to pride myself on quick, logical decisions: the green shoes or the teal? Now I stare slack-jawed at the shoe store and go home with six different colors. Spouse thinks I'm indecisive, but I'm just not sure.

May 10

Faith is taking the first step even when
we don't see the whole staircase.
MARTIN LUTHER KING JR.

May 11

YEAR

YEAR

YEAR

YEAR

YEAR

Time to LOL!
Learn creative coping techniques and calm fretful spirits through bite-sized, digestible doses of the Bread of Life. Maybe a hunk of Godiva, too!

May 12

If we only do as much as we can do, then the
Lord will take over and do what only He can do.

May 13

YEAR

YEAR

YEAR

YEAR

YEAR

"A cheerful heart is good medicine,
but a crushed spirit dries up the bones."
PROVERBS 17:22 NIV

What does Proverbs 17:22 tell us about the importance of having fun?

May 14

YEAR

YEAR

YEAR

YEAR

YEAR

Today, kick seriousness out for the evening and plan a night
of hysteria. Include the people and things (foods, games,
movies, goofy clothes) that make you smile and indulge in a
little hilarity. I'll bet your stress level will drop five floors!

May 15

YEAR
....
....
....
....
....
....

YEAR
....
....
....
....
....
....

YEAR
....
....
....
....
....
....

YEAR
....
....
....
....
....
....

YEAR
....
....
....
....
....

Time to LOL!
Knowing about God and knowing God is the same difference
between reading a cordon bleu recipe and being Julia Child.

May 16

Love is kind and patient, never jealous, boastful, proud, or rude.
Love isn't selfish or quick tempered. It doesn't keep a record of
wrongs that others do. Love rejoices in the truth, but not in evil.
1 CORINTHIANS 13:4–6 CEV

May 17

YEAR

YEAR

YEAR

YEAR

YEAR

In the many laugh-or-cry crises that crowd our days,
thank You, Lord, for helping us choose to laugh!

May 18

YEAR

YEAR

YEAR

YEAR

YEAR

Worship doesn't have to be just in a stained-glass building
or magnificent cathedral or at a designated hour or location.
The true church isn't the edifice. . .it's us, you and me.

May 19

Have you ever been so moved that you burst forth
in spontaneous worship? If not, you should try it
sometime. . .there's nothing so exhilarating!

May 20

YEAR

YEAR

YEAR

YEAR

YEAR

Don't hit back; discover beauty in everyone.
ROMANS 12:17 MSG

May 21

YEAR

YEAR

YEAR

YEAR

YEAR

You are not superwoman with nerves of steel. Or guts either.
Stress is kryptonite, and it's out to rip off your cape and reduce you
to a pile of quivering, ineffective mush. Okay, that's the bad news.
How about some good? . . . When stress gets the best of us,
the heavenly Father is there to put you back together again.

May 22

YEAR
....
....
....
....

YEAR
....
....
....
....

YEAR
....
....
....
....

YEAR
....
....
....
....

YEAR
....
....
....
....

Add yourself to your daily to-do list. . . .
You're important!

May 23

Time to LOL!
Side effects of a late-afternoon nap can include an
interesting maze of facial furrows from the pile of
unfolded laundry upon which your head lands.

May 24

YEAR

YEAR

YEAR

YEAR

YEAR

We will tell the next generation the praiseworthy deeds of the Lord, his power, and the wonders he has done.
PSALM 78:4 NIV

May 25

YEAR

....

....

....

....

YEAR

....

....

....

....

YEAR

....

....

....

....

YEAR

....

....

....

....

YEAR

....

....

....

....

Time to LOL!
God's divinely orchestrated levity of love plays out all around
us through His marvelous creation: take, for example,
aardvarks, spoonbill platypuses, and cowlicks.

May 26

Time to LOL!

Repetitive redundancy. No, this is not the name of a new rock group.
It's what you should do to take your frantic self down a notch:
crochet, do needlepoint, play piano scales. . . You need a calm, repetitive,
manual task that takes minimal brain power.
Chopping firewood doesn't count.

May 27

YEAR

YEAR

YEAR

YEAR

YEAR

We should learn from our mistakes, sure, but then shed the guilt like a
moth-eaten winter coat. Don a fresh spring outfit and look ahead.
Our past prepares us for the future if we're open to the present.

May 28

YEAR

YEAR

YEAR

YEAR

YEAR

I will sing for joy at the works of Your hands.
PSALM 92:4 NASB

May 29

Take a moment and praise our Lord and Savior for His
all-powerful sovereignty. Remember, He's large and in charge!

May 30

YEAR

YEAR

YEAR

YEAR

YEAR

Negativity is habit-forming. . . . Channeling Eeyore becomes the soundtrack for our subconscious thoughts. Those mopey, self-depreciating donkey thoughts wear us down and wear us out before we even realize the source of the erosion. Why settle for defeat when, with a few minor attitude adjustments, we could open the door for *amazing* possibilities?

May 31

YEAR

YEAR

YEAR

YEAR

YEAR

Time to LOL!
In my humble but accurate opinion, naps are
an essential pause in the nonstop stress of our day.
When I miss my nappy, ain't nobody happy.

June 1

YEAR

YEAR

YEAR

YEAR

YEAR

A man's counsel is sweet to his friend.
PROVERBS 27:9 NASB

June 2

YEAR

YEAR

YEAR

YEAR

YEAR

Shake the mental Etch-A-Sketch. Get out the attitude chainsaw. . . .
Replace negative thoughts with a positive spin.

June 3

Tack on hope. Add the magical three-letter word, *yet*. When tacked on at the end of a negative thought, it miraculously transforms "I can't" perspectives into "I can, with a little more time."

June 4

YEAR

....
....
....
....
....

YEAR

....
....
....
....
....

YEAR

....
....
....
....
....

YEAR

....
....
....
....
....

YEAR

....
....
....
....

Think a moment of the top three negative messages you routinely send yourself. Now practice tweaking your tone, speaking like your own BFF, and tacking on hope. Take the bold step from negative to positive thinking!

June 5

Love wisdom like a sister.
PROVERBS 7:4 NLT

June 6

Love has nothing to do with what you are expecting to get—
only with what you are expecting to give—which is everything.
KATHERINE HEPBURN

June 7

YEAR

YEAR

YEAR

YEAR

YEAR

Time to LOL!
Opportunity knocks softly, but temptation parks
its fat derriere on the doorbell, scarfing chocolate.

June 8

Walk, run, ski, work out, join the roller derby—whatever waxes
your eyebrows, but make exercise a priority. Do it for *you*.

June 9

YEAR

YEAR

YEAR

YEAR

YEAR

The troubles of my heart are enlarged;
bring me out of my distresses.
PSALM 25:17 NASB

June 10

YEAR

YEAR

YEAR

YEAR

YEAR

Concern draws us to God.
Worry pulls us from Him.
JOANNA WEAVER

June 11

God doesn't want us to be washed-out dishrags. God is not glorified when we are so exhausted that we can't tell we're brushing our hair with a toothbrush or trying to pay for groceries with our frequent shopper card. . . . Scale down, pull back, and simplify.

June 12

YEAR

YEAR

YEAR

YEAR

YEAR

Read the instructions! Make a plan and stick to it in reading and studying God's Word daily. This is how we replenish our depleted reserves.

June 13

Then, because you belong to Christ Jesus, God will bless
you with peace that no one can completely understand.
And this peace will control the way you think and feel.
PHILIPPIANS 4:7 CEV

June 14

YEAR

....
....
....
....
....

YEAR

....
....
....
....
....

YEAR

....
....
....
....
....

YEAR

....
....
....
....
....

YEAR

....
....
....
....

As adults, we don't often have the luxury of free hours,
but we can carve free minutes out of each day if we diligently
simplify and unclog those constipated calendars. That, dear sister,
is when we reconnect with that summer morning feeling.

June 15

YEAR

....
....
....
....
....

YEAR

....
....
....
....
....

YEAR

....
....
....
....
....

YEAR

....
....
....
....
....

YEAR

....
....
....
....

Lord, help me remember the worst thing that could possibly happen to
me today is that I'd wake up in heaven in Your arms. That's exciting!

June 16

YEAR

....
....
....
....
....

YEAR

....
....
....
....
....

YEAR

....
....
....
....
....

YEAR

....
....
....
....
....

YEAR

....
....
....
....

Over the years I have honed the art of worry into a science.
I've systematically and diligently transformed molehills into mountains.
I've whipped pesky irritants into frothy, acetic colon-coaters and fretted
over annoying burdens until they invaded my dreams.

June 17

YEAR

YEAR

YEAR

YEAR

YEAR

Weeping may stay for the night,
but rejoicing comes in the morning.
PSALM 30:5 NIV

June 18

The Lord doesn't ask us to understand;
He only asks us to trust.

June 19

YEAR

....
....
....
....
....

YEAR

....
....
....
....
....

YEAR

....
....
....
....
....

YEAR

....
....
....
....
....

YEAR

....
....
....
....
....

Laughter is our lifeline when we're sinking into the pit
of rigidity, when we're so absorbed in the stressful
details of our lives that we're missing the fun.

June 20

Time to LOL!
I heard on the radio that scientists have discovered a natural extract in chocolate that cleans teeth better than toothpaste. Hey, I'll bite!

June 21

YEAR

YEAR

YEAR

YEAR

YEAR

Love never gives up, never loses faith, is always hopeful,
and endures through every circumstance.
1 CORINTHIANS 13:7 NLT

June 22

Jesus came to earth as the Creator in created form.
He loves us *that* much!

June 23

In order to change my behavior, I first have to change
my way of thinking. The way I act starts with what's
happening in my head. No stinkin' thinkin' for me!

June 24

YEAR

YEAR

YEAR

YEAR

Are you overextending yourself? Spreading your time or energies too thin? Regardless of how well-intentioned we are, we're only human and the Master Designer, who created us and *knows* our limitations, wants us to set parameters, to pick and choose the way we expend our finite energies.

June 25

YEAR

....
....
....
....

YEAR

....
....
....
....

YEAR

....
....
....
....

YEAR

....
....
....
....

YEAR

....
....
....
....

For God has not given us a spirit of fear and timidity,
but of power, love, and self-discipline.
2 TIMOTHY 1:7 NLT

June 26

YEAR

YEAR

YEAR

YEAR

YEAR

Make daily time with Papa God a priority.
Tight schedules are no excuse.

June 27

YEAR

YEAR

YEAR

YEAR

YEAR

Consistently refresh your reserves—your level of dependency on God's grace and patience is reflected in your grace and patience toward others.

June 28

Time to LOL!
Bette Davis was right:
"Old age ain't no place for sissies."

June 29

"Call on me and come and pray to me,
and I will listen to you."
JEREMIAH 29:12 NIV

YEAR

YEAR

YEAR

YEAR

YEAR

God's in the miracle business, and He "*is* able to do far more abundantly
beyond all that we ask or think, according to the power that works
within us" (Ephesians 3:20 NASB, emphasis added). That power,
of course, is His enormous, undefeatable power.

July 1

Time to LOL!
A wonderful definition of feminine might: True strength is breaking a
chocolate bar into four pieces bare-handed. . .and then eating only one.

July 2

YEAR

YEAR

YEAR

YEAR

YEAR

I know God will not give me anything I can't handle.
I just wish He didn't trust me so much.
MOTHER TERESA

July 3

YEAR

YEAR

YEAR

YEAR

YEAR

Pray without ceasing.
1 THESSALONIANS 5:17 NASB

July 4

YEAR

YEAR

YEAR

YEAR

YEAR

Time to LOL!

I think as women assume greater authority in the scientific community,
there will be more evidence unearthed proving that chocolate
should be included as one of the basic food groups.

July 5

YEAR

YEAR

YEAR

YEAR

YEAR

What's the answer for us matrons of muddle? . . . We must lower our expectations. That's right, pitch perfectionism, lose the legalism, cast off comparisons. Limbo under that self-imposed bar of spotlessness!

July 6

YEAR

YEAR

YEAR

YEAR

YEAR

God wants us to invest our precious minutes on earth
in people, not things. Focus on pursuing those
whose souls hang in the balance of eternity.

July 7

YEAR

YEAR

YEAR

YEAR

YEAR

We can make our plans,
but the LORD determines our steps.
PROVERBS 16:9 NLT

July 8

YEAR

YEAR

YEAR

YEAR

YEAR

Faith can move mountains, but don't
be surprised if God hands you a shovel.
UNKNOWN

July 9

YEAR

YEAR

YEAR

YEAR

YEAR

Pride is an underhanded thief. It sneaks up and robs us of the heart-changing gratitude that is a byproduct of knowing—and acknowledging—that our attributes, abilities, and accolades are simply gifts for our Creator. Gifts wrapped in love and tied with a bow of grace.

July 10

YEAR

YEAR

YEAR

YEAR

YEAR

When you get to the end of your rope,
you'll find Papa God waiting with a ladder.

July 11

Nothing in all creation is hidden from God's sight.
HEBREWS 4:13 NIV

July 12

YEAR

YEAR

YEAR

YEAR

YEAR

Why does God care about stubborn, rebellious creatures?
Why should He waste His time rescuing hapless victims of their
own bad choices? We certainly don't deserve His mercy. Yet He
lovingly extends it to us anyway. Over and over and over again.

July 13

YEAR

YEAR

YEAR

YEAR

YEAR

Receiving Papa God's mercy is like opening a note from someone
you've offended and finding a five-hundred-dollar gift card to your
favorite shoe store. When was the last time you experienced
His incomprehensible mercy and forgiveness?

July 14

YEAR

YEAR

YEAR

YEAR

YEAR

Time to LOL!
I've found that a big ole hunk of peanut butter fudge is
the best way to gag that obnoxious skinny inner gal
trying to bust through the waist rolls.

July 15

YEAR

YEAR

YEAR

YEAR

YEAR

"If you had faith even as small as a mustard seed,
you could say to this mountain, 'Move from here to there,'
and it would move. Nothing would be impossible."
MATTHEW 17:20 NLT

July 16

YEAR

YEAR

YEAR

YEAR

YEAR

Colossians 2:7 advises us to "Let your lives be built on him. . .
and you will overflow with thankfulness" (NLT). What steps
can you take to make living thankfully an everyday habit?

July 17

YEAR

YEAR

YEAR

YEAR

YEAR

In the midst of my rushed IM life, Lord, give me patience
to wait on You to act in Your own perfect timing.

July 18

YEAR

YEAR

YEAR

YEAR

YEAR

Time to LOL!
Isn't it simply polite to answer when certain foods call our name?

July 19

YEAR

YEAR

YEAR

YEAR

YEAR

The LORD is my shepherd, I shall not want. . . .
Your rod and Your staff, they comfort me.
PSALM 23:1, 4 NASB

July 20

YEAR

YEAR

YEAR

YEAR

YEAR

Living water: Why settle for a trickle when
God wants to give you Niagara Falls?

July 21

Papa God, help me show by my actions that
what's important to You is important to me.

July 22

YEAR

YEAR

YEAR

YEAR

YEAR

Joy and laughter are soul sisters;
they travel together.

July 23

You, LORD, are. . .the One who lifts my head high.
PSALM 3:3 NIV

July 24

YEAR

YEAR

YEAR

YEAR

YEAR

Time to LOL!
Sometimes I wish I'd grabbed the
glue stick instead of my lipstick.

July 25

Time to LOL!
It must've been a woman who coined the
phrase "wee hours" on a midnight potty run.

July 26

The more I've watched the connection between humor
and creativity, the more I've realized there is very little
difference between the terms, "Aha!" and "Ha Ha!"

VATCHE BARTEKIAN, STRESS MANAGEMENT SPECIALIST

July 27

YEAR

YEAR

YEAR

YEAR

YEAR

Be anxious for nothing, but in everything by prayer and supplication with thanksgiving let your requests be made known to God. And the peace of God, which surpasses all comprehension, will guard your hearts and your minds in Christ Jesus.

PHILIPPIANS 4:6–7 NASB

July 28

YEAR

YEAR

YEAR

YEAR

Time to LOL!
I suffer from CDD: Chocolate Deficit Disorder. A choco-infusion
every two hours is necessary for temperament stability
and the mental health of those around me.

July 29

YEAR

YEAR

YEAR

YEAR

YEAR

Our Lord specializes in repairing rips in relationships. He's more than happy to provide the cord strength when two of the strands become frayed.

July 30

YEAR

YEAR

YEAR

YEAR

YEAR

You don't have to like someone to pray for them. But you may
be surprised how bitterness evolves into something
quite different when you're on your knees.

July 31

YEAR

YEAR

YEAR

YEAR

YEAR

*I am leaving you with a gift—peace of mind and heart. And the peace
I give is a gift the world cannot give. So don't be troubled or afraid.*
JOHN 14:27 NLT

August 1

YEAR

YEAR

YEAR

YEAR

YEAR

Wonder is involuntary praise.
EDWARD YOUNG

YEAR

....
....
....
....
....
....

YEAR

....
....
....
....
....
....

YEAR

....
....
....
....
....
....

YEAR

....
....
....
....
....
....

YEAR

....
....
....
....
....

Lord, teach me that to You, I am beautiful, beloved, and of great worth.
All other measuring sticks are just wood.

August 3

Our heavenly Father doesn't care how much we know,
but He wants to know how much we care.

August 4

YEAR

YEAR

YEAR

YEAR

YEAR

And God will wipe the tears from every face.
ISAIAH 25:8 MSG

August 5

YEAR

YEAR

YEAR

YEAR

YEAR

Time to LOL!
Let she who is guiltless cast the first stone. Who hasn't stashed
Tootsie Rolls among the potted plants or hidden M&Ms in her
ibuprofen bottle? Or buried telltale Snickers wrappers
inside balled up paper towels in the trash can?

August 6

YEAR

YEAR

YEAR

YEAR

Time to LOL!
There must be a way to use gravity to our advantage.
Maybe ditching our bras would pull the wrinkles out of our faces.

August 7

YEAR
....

YEAR
....

YEAR
....

YEAR
....

YEAR
....

Lord, help me live my life out loud, like the melodic
crescendo of a beautiful orchestra. Not a foghorn.

August 8

Be sure of this: I am with you always,
even to the end of the age.
MATTHEW 28:20 NLT

August 9

YEAR

YEAR

YEAR

YEAR

YEAR

Boogie. Belly dance. Polka. Get your bad self down. Music has the magical
ability to speed us up, calm us down, distract (in a good way),
and inspire us—tap into this simple source of happiness (pun intended)!

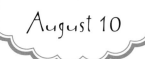

August 10

YEAR
....

YEAR
....

YEAR
....

YEAR
....

YEAR
....

Sometimes prayer is all it takes to transform loathing into loving.

August 11

YEAR

YEAR

YEAR

YEAR

YEAR

It's so hard to ask for directions when we get lost.
But Papa God is standing there beside the road holding
the map; we just have to stop and roll down the window.

August 12

*I sought the LORD and He answered me
and delivered me from all my fears.*
PSALM 34:4 NASB

August 13

It's tempting to pray for the elimination of obstacles in our lives,
but the creek would never dance if Papa God removed the rocks.

August 14

Papa God is our heavenly Father and we can trust that He will get us safely where we need to be. We don't need to worry, fret, or fear the what-ifs.

August 15

Trust is the antidote to anxiety; it's the
resolution of worry and the destruction of fear.
JAMES MacDONALD

August 16

Come near to God and he will come near to you.
JAMES 4:8 NIV

August 17

YEAR

YEAR

YEAR

YEAR

YEAR

Remember, the almighty Creator of the universe set
the precedent by resting after a strenuous workweek.

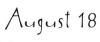

August 18

YEAR

....
....
....
....
....
....

YEAR

....
....
....
....
....
....

YEAR

....
....
....
....
....
....

YEAR

....
....
....
....
....
....

YEAR

....
....
....

Time to LOL!

I recently read that our personalities are reflected in our snacks of
choice. . . . Hey, maybe instead of the traditional four personality
types (choleric, sanguine, melancholic, and phlegmatic),
we should switch to tortilla, pretzel, cheese curl, or potato chip.
Women would certainly understand the implications better.

August 19

YEAR

YEAR

YEAR

YEAR

YEAR

Infinite possibilities. . .are born of faith.
MOTHER TERESA

August 20

YEAR

YEAR

YEAR

YEAR

YEAR

Wait patiently for the LORD.
Be brave and courageous.
PSALM 27:14 NLT

August 21

Do you know the one stress reliever that women need every day but
often neglect? Nope, it's not love, sex, or chocolate engorgement. . .
Are you ready? It's fun! That's right—good ole giggle-producing,
endorphin-generating, tension-popping fun!

August 22

Why don't we dance more? Even dignified prophetess Miriam
grabbed her tambourine and cut loose with her girlfriends.
I, too, want to hear God's music and do His celebration dance.

August 23

Girlfriends are the way we hone our Christlikeness.

August 24

YEAR

....
....
....
....
....

YEAR

....
....
....
....
....

YEAR

....
....
....
....
....

YEAR

....
....
....
....
....

YEAR

....
....
....
....
....

In peace I will both lie down and sleep.
PSALM 4:8 NASB

August 25

YEAR

YEAR

YEAR

YEAR

YEAR

Time to LOL!
These earth suits are only temporary. Heaven will not have beauty pageants. And I really don't think it would be heaven without Oreos.

August 26

YEAR

....
....
....
....
....
....

YEAR

....
....
....
....
....
....

YEAR

....
....
....
....
....
....

YEAR

....
....
....
....
....
....

YEAR

....
....
....
....
....

Papa God wants us to be tender in surrender,
not to rule like a mule.

August 27

God is just as sovereign today as He was in biblical times. He's in control of each and every detail of our lives. And the peace of God, which surpasses all human understanding, will keep our hearts and our minds out of the anxiety stress-pool.

August 28

YEAR

YEAR

YEAR

YEAR

YEAR

*We know that God is always at work
for the good of everyone who loves him.*
ROMANS 8:28 CEV

August 29

YEAR

YEAR

YEAR

YEAR

YEAR

Prayers are verbal faith.

August 30

YEAR

YEAR

YEAR

YEAR

Time to LOL!
Ulcer is *kids* spelled backward.
Well, it should be anyway.

August 31

My best stress reliever has been to remind myself in the midst of the fray that the most important things in my world are my people. *My* peeps. Those beautiful souls God has entrusted to my care for a few short years.

September 1

YEAR

YEAR

YEAR

YEAR

YEAR

Rest in the LORD and wait patiently for Him.
PSALM 37:7 NASB

September 2

YEAR

....

....

....

....

....

YEAR

....

....

....

....

....

YEAR

....

....

....

....

....

YEAR

....

....

....

....

....

YEAR

....

....

....

....

Time to LOL!
The way I see it, I'm actually being thoughtful by ignoring
my mop and dust rag. I'm eliminating the sinful temptation
for friends who might fall short in comparison.

September 3

When I'm plugged into Your power source, Lord, it's amazing
how long I can march while beating my big drum!

September 4

YEAR

YEAR

YEAR

YEAR

YEAR

Time to LOL!
I really don't think it would be heaven without chocolate chip cookies.

September 5

YEAR

....
....
....
....
....
....

YEAR

....
....
....
....
....
....

YEAR

....
....
....
....
....
....

YEAR

....
....
....
....
....
....

YEAR

....
....
....
....
....
....

*My flesh and my heart may fail, but God is the
strength of my heart and my portion forever.*
PSALM 73:26 NASB

September 6

YEAR

YEAR

YEAR

YEAR

YEAR

I've come to realize Jesus was absolutely right in Luke 12 (big *duh*—isn't He always right?) . . . "Has anyone by fussing before the mirror ever gotten taller by so much as an inch? If fussing can't even do that, why fuss at all? (MSG). I mean really, what's all the fuss about?

September 7

YEAR

YEAR

YEAR

YEAR

YEAR

Generosity is faith with legs.

September 8

YEAR

....
....
....
....
....

YEAR

....
....
....
....
....

YEAR

....
....
....
....
....

YEAR

....
....
....
....
....

YEAR

....
....
....

Caving to the dark side doesn't *have* to be our destiny, Luke!
We have the Force above all other forces, the one true,
living God, willing and able to provide armor (for defense) and
ammo (for offense) in our ongoing battle against temptation.

September 9

YEAR

YEAR

YEAR

YEAR

YEAR

Resist the devil and he will flee from you.
JAMES 4:7 NASB

September 10

YEAR

YEAR

YEAR

YEAR

YEAR

God's love for us isn't dependent on anything we do or don't do, blab or omit. Our Father's love itself is what makes us whole and holy; not anything we can contrive, create, or earn.

September 11

YEAR

YEAR

YEAR

YEAR

YEAR

In what specific ways does Papa God's unconditional
love make you feel cuddled, cherished, peaceful?

September 12

YEAR

YEAR

YEAR

YEAR

YEAR

An ounce of mother is worth a pound of clergy.
SPANISH PROVERB

September 13

"No eye has seen, no ear has heard, and no mind has imagined what God has prepared for those who love him."
1 CORINTHIANS 2:9 NLT

September 14

Certain thoughts are prayers. There are moments when,
whatever be the attitude of the body, the soul is on its knees.
VICTOR HUGO, *LES MISÉRABLES*

September 15

YEAR

YEAR

YEAR

YEAR

YEAR

I don't want to approach prayer as a chore. I'm not reporting for duty
or giving God instructions on what's best for me. Nor do I want my
prayer life to consist merely of rhino-in-the-road desperation pleas to
NeedGodNOW.com. . . . I come with a humble heart, an open mind,
and a thirsty spirit. I *cherish* spending time with Him.

September 16

YEAR

YEAR

YEAR

YEAR

YEAR

Is prayer more of a single event or a continuous mind-set for you?
Prayer can become our last resort rather than our first resort if we
don't regard communication with Christ as important as breathing.
Even before our prayers are answered, we benefit from
the immense blessing of His loving company.

September 17

YEAR

YEAR

YEAR

YEAR

YEAR

You can be sure that God will take care of everything you need, his generosity exceeding even yours in the glory that pours from Jesus.
PHILIPPIANS 4:19–20 MSG

September 18

YEAR

YEAR

YEAR

YEAR

YEAR

It's a crying shame to devote our lives to the goal of standing at
the door to eternity with gorgeous size 4 bodies, tanned to perfection,
foreheads silky-smooth, eyes bag-free, hair gleaming, arms Dumbo
flapless, thighs tapioca-free. What good is it? God will not be impressed.
He'll be looking at our insides, at our hearts.

September 19

It's humbling and incredibly encouraging to know
the Creator of the universe somehow finds the time to
manage even the smallest details of our lives. It makes it
much easier to trust Him with the big stuff, doesn't it?

September 20

YEAR

YEAR

YEAR

YEAR

YEAR

The Master Potter loves even us cracked pots. To Him, we're not worse or inferior to Ming or Tiffany. . .just different. Practical instead of pricey, useful instead of ornamental, and exquisitely lovely in our own right.

September 21

YEAR

YEAR

YEAR

YEAR

YEAR

Life is made up of little accomplishments;
these are what we should make a *big* deal about.

September 22

YEAR

YEAR

YEAR

YEAR

YEAR

Master of the universe, who calmed the stormy seas, send me
a chill pill when problems seem unfixable. Remind me that
everyday miracles are Your thing. It's what You do.

September 23

Time to LOL!

One of the most important and long-lasting relationships we must cultivate is with these earth suits God has entrusted to us for a limited time. Depending on the condition in which we maintain them, our bodies can be warmly comforting, a source of pleasure, a vehicle for adventure, or a painfully restrictive straitjacket.

September 24

Let's admit it—none of us wants our temples to fall into ruins.
With a sturdy foundation of prevention and a slap or two of
maintenance mortar, our flesh and blood cathedrals can glorify
God for decades to come without one brick crumbling from neglect.

September 25

YEAR

YEAR

YEAR

YEAR

YEAR

We are the temple of the living God.
2 CORINTHIANS 6:16 NIV

September 26

Has your focus been on decorating your earth suit? What steps can you take to shift emphasis to the inside rather than the outside?

September 27

God can make anyone into anything. He made ninety-year-old
Sarah a mother and Rahab, a prostitute, an honored ancestor
of Jesus. He morphed a lonely little Jewish orphan into gorgeous
Queen Esther. And He's not finished with me yet!

September 28

YEAR

YEAR

YEAR

YEAR

YEAR

When I start to worry or obsess, I recite the facts I know to be true:
God is in control; He loves me; He wants what's best for me, even
though my ideas may not be His; I only find peace by resting in His will.

September 29

YEAR

....

....

....

....

....

YEAR

....

....

....

....

....

YEAR

....

....

....

....

....

YEAR

....

....

....

....

....

YEAR

....

....

....

....

....

*God, the source of hope, will fill you completely with joy and
peace because you trust in him. Then you will overflow with
confident hope through the power of the Holy Spirit.*
ROMANS 15:13 NLT

September 30

Papa God never meant for us to keep going nine hundred miles per hour all day. He built triggers into our bodies to cue us when it's time to escape consciousness. Wise people listen to those cues, such as notable nappers Albert Einstein, Thomas Edison, Winston Churchill, John F. Kennedy, and Ronald Reagan.

October 1

YEAR

YEAR

YEAR

YEAR

YEAR

Jesus said, "Let's go off by ourselves to a quiet place and rest awhile."
He said this because there were so many people coming and going that
Jesus and his apostles didn't even have time to eat. So they left by
boat for a quiet place, where they could be alone (MARK 6:30–32 NLT).
Why do you think stealing away for rest was so important to Jesus?
Why should it be important to you?

October 2

My determination is to transfer this habit of worry into
an instant moment of prayer and leaving it with God.
CHARLES SWINDOLL

October 3

YEAR

YEAR

YEAR

YEAR

YEAR

How blessed is the man who trusts in You.
PSALM 84:12 NASB

October 4

YEAR

YEAR

YEAR

YEAR

YEAR

The nice thing about the future
is that it always starts tomorrow.
UNKNOWN

October 5

The Bible says our bodies are God's temples. If we, as temple caretakers, are to withstand battering gales and the onslaught of relentless enemy attacks, we must fortify our living structures from within!

October 6

YEAR

....
....
....
....
....
....

YEAR

....
....
....
....
....
....

YEAR

....
....
....
....
....
....

YEAR

....
....
....
....
....
....

YEAR

....
....
....
....
....

There are no coincidences in the grace notes of our lives. Grace notes—
the little daily special touches from Papa God that let us know He's got
our backs—are the everyday miracles that reflect God's sovereignty,
His supreme power and authority over every detail or our lives.

October 7

YEAR

YEAR

YEAR

YEAR

YEAR

When we turn control of our lives over to our Lord, everlasting life is ours. Not just the promise of heaven when we die, but the glorious opportunity to live our lives walking beside our Abba Father, our Papa God, *today*.

October 8

Developing patience is like an oyster creating a rare pearl—
we shouldn't pray for it unless we're prepared to
withstand the long grit-grinding process that produces it.

October 9

We know how much God loves us,
and we have put our trust in his love.
1 JOHN 4:16 NLT

October 10

YEAR

YEAR

YEAR

YEAR

YEAR

As grown women, the what-ifs often steal our peace and add to our emotional turmoil. . . . We must remind ourselves that the what-ifs aren't real. That's Satan sticking his dirty, rotten fingers into our hearts and minds to steal the peace Papa God promises if we depend on Him.

October 11

*Be on your guard and stay awake. Your enemy, the devil,
is like a roaring lion, sneaking around to find someone to attack.*
1 PETER 5:8 CEV

October 12

YEAR

YEAR

YEAR

YEAR

YEAR

Jesus is not just our Messiah, Prince of Peace,
and Savior. He's our role model as a human facing real,
heart-slamming adversity, our "God in a bod."

October 13

YEAR

YEAR

YEAR

YEAR

YEAR

Our heavenly Father looks past our crusty outside trappings to our soft,
sensitive underbellies, where we were created in His image.

October 14

YEAR

YEAR

YEAR

YEAR

YEAR

P: Placing
E: Each
A: Aggravation at
C: Christ's feet. . .
E: Expectantly!

October 15

Why, my soul, are you downcast? . . .
Put your hope in God, for I will yet praise him.
PSALM 42:11 NIV

October 16

If, for whatever reason, we can't remove a temptation,
we must remove *ourselves* from the temptation. Get thee out of
there, girl! Don't stand nekked in front of a speeding freight train!

October 17

YEAR

YEAR

YEAR

YEAR

YEAR

God measures our success by faithfulness, not results.
Aren't you glad He cares more about the ingredients
than whether the soufflé flopped?

October 18

YEAR

YEAR

YEAR

YEAR

YEAR

Our Creator is standing by with a life preserver as we tread water
in the stress-pool of everyday life. That buoyant ring meant to hold
our heads above water is our Father's inexplicable, infilling peace.

October 19

YEAR

YEAR

YEAR

YEAR

YEAR

My peace I give you. I do not give to you as the world gives.
Do not let your hearts be troubled and do not be afraid.
JOHN 14:27 NIV

October 20

YEAR

YEAR

YEAR

YEAR

YEAR

You gain strength, courage, and confidence by every experience
in which you really stop to look fear in the face. You must
do the thing which you think you cannot do.

ELEANOR ROOSEVELT

October 21

YEAR

YEAR

YEAR

YEAR

YEAR

Time to LOL!
Containing joy is like trying to repress the freckle gene.

October 22

YEAR

YEAR

YEAR

YEAR

YEAR

If God used Balaam's donkey and Peter's
rooster to do His work, He can use me, too!

October 23

Quiet down before God, be prayerful before him.
PSALM 37:7 MSG

October 24

YEAR

YEAR

YEAR

YEAR

YEAR

Sometimes failure is Papa God's way of saying,
"Wait, My child. . .this just isn't the right time."

October 25

YEAR

_____

YEAR

_____

YEAR

_____

YEAR

_____

YEAR

_____

What good are spiritual gifts if we stuff them in our
closets or underneath our beds and never open them?

October 26

YEAR

YEAR

YEAR

YEAR

YEAR

Have you ever lost something, then found it right in front of you? Life is like that. We search for answers and get uptight and stressed out when the source of knowledge is in our possession the whole time. It's called the Bible.

October 27

YEAR

YEAR

YEAR

YEAR

YEAR

So let's not get tired of doing what is good. At just the right time we will reap a harvest of blessing if we don't give up
GALATIANS 6:9 NLT

October 28

The things I've found that once were lost become oh, so much more precious. Like faith. And German chocolate. *Mmm.*

October 29

I worship the Creator of butterflies, humpback whales, three-toed sloths, puppies, rainbows, waterfalls, and sunbeams. How can I *not* smile?

October 30

YEAR

YEAR

YEAR

YEAR

YEAR

God had us—you and me—in mind to be the focus of His love even before the creation of the world. What a calming, reassuring thought!

October 31

YEAR

....

....

....

....

....

YEAR

....

....

....

....

....

YEAR

....

....

....

....

....

YEAR

....

....

....

....

....

YEAR

....

....

....

....

....

*Long before he laid down earth's foundations, he had us
in mind, had settled on us as the focus of his love,
to be made whole and holy by his love.*
EPHESIANS 1:4 MSG

November 1

YEAR

YEAR

YEAR

YEAR

YEAR

Time to LOL!
No diet will remove all the fat from your body because the
brain is entirely fat. Without a brain, you might look good,
but all you could do is run for public office.
GEORGE BERNARD SHAW

November 2

Life isn't always fair, but God is always God.

November 3

YEAR

YEAR

YEAR

YEAR

YEAR

Never forget that the best stress reliever we have is each other!

November 4

YEAR

....
....
....
....
....

YEAR

....
....
....
....

YEAR

....
....
....
....

YEAR

....
....
....
....

YEAR

....
....
....
....

He will cover you with his feathers,
and under his wings you will find refuge.
PSALM 91:4 NIV

November 5

YEAR

YEAR

YEAR

YEAR

YEAR

Peace, in the midst of life's chaos. Peace, that jumping-off platform for inexplicable joy. Peace, that illusive, anxiety-free place of freedom we long for. . . Only when our trust is anchored in God can we find peace.

November 6

YEAR

....

....

....

....

....

YEAR

....

....

....

....

....

YEAR

....

....

....

....

....

YEAR

....

....

....

....

....

YEAR

....

....

....

....

Even sawed-off stumps will eventually become majestic,
towering evergreens if they just keep sending out sprouts.

November 7

YEAR

YEAR

YEAR

YEAR

YEAR

Lord, help me remember that today I can either
influence others toward Christ. . .or repel them.

November 8

We must get rid of everything that slows us down,
especially the sin that just won't let go. And we must
be determined to run the race that is ahead of us.
HEBREWS 12:1 CEV

November 9

YEAR

YEAR

YEAR

YEAR

Our BFF is there for us through svelte and bloated, sweet and grumpy, thoughtful and insensitive. How much more can we count on our Blessed Friend Forever—Papa God—to be there for us?

November 10

YEAR

YEAR

YEAR

YEAR

YEAR

A hope-filled person will realize that abundant life in Christ isn't about simply enduring the storm but also about learning to dance in the puddles. Let's grab our galoshes and boogie!

November 11

YEAR

YEAR

YEAR

YEAR

YEAR

Remember how to laugh. A real, honest-to-goodness, gurgling-from-the-guts giggle. The kind that acts as a catalyst to release the joy of the Lord in your soul and color your future with hope for a better tomorrow.

November 12

YEAR

YEAR

YEAR

YEAR

YEAR

You will keep in perfect peace all who trust in you,
all whose thoughts are fixed on you!
ISAIAH 26:3 NLT

November 13

YEAR

YEAR

YEAR

YEAR

Never give up! David picked up five stones,
not just one, when he went out to face Goliath!

November 14

YEAR

YEAR

YEAR

YEAR

YEAR

You can straighten your posture and adjust your face, but if
the change doesn't come from the inside out, it won't stick.
God is our Interior Decorator. Only He can provide that
inner joy that projects outward and lifts our heads.

November 15

YEAR

YEAR

YEAR

YEAR

YEAR

When trouble squeezes me like a toothpaste tube,
I pray that grace is what oozes out.

November 16

YEAR

....

....

....

....

YEAR

....

....

....

....

YEAR

....

....

....

....

YEAR

....

....

....

....

YEAR

....

....

....

For the LORD your God is living among you. He is a mighty savior.
He will take delight in you with gladness. With his love, he will
calm all your fears. He will rejoice over you with joyful songs.
ZEPHANIAH 3:17 NLT

November 17

YEAR

YEAR

YEAR

YEAR

YEAR

God is in the business of using tiny slivers of what's left over to do mighty things. He accomplishes amazing miracles with remnants!

November 18

Prayer is not just spiritual punctuation;
it's every word of our life's story.

November 19

YEAR

YEAR

YEAR

YEAR

Prayer is the least and the most we can do.

November 20

YEAR

YEAR

YEAR

YEAR

YEAR

*Laugh with your happy friends when they're happy;
share tears when they're down.*
ROMANS 12:15 MSG

November 21

YEAR

YEAR

YEAR

YEAR

Time to LOL!
Weight control is no piece of cake. You know it's true:
sugar shows and money talks, but chocolate sings!

November 22

YEAR

YEAR

YEAR

YEAR

YEAR

God's specialty is in making positives from negatives. In His garden of life,
cow-patty fertilizer produces glorious flower blossoms.

November 23

YEAR

....
....
....
....
....

YEAR

....
....
....
....
....

YEAR

....
....
....
....
....

YEAR

....
....
....
....
....

YEAR

....
....
....
....
....

Can you think of five things to be grateful for this very minute?

November 24

YEAR

YEAR

YEAR

YEAR

Cease striving *and know that I am God.*
PSALM 46:10 NASB

November 25

YEAR

YEAR

YEAR

YEAR

YEAR

It is not enough for a man to pray cream and live skim milk.
HENRY WARD BEECHER

November 26

YEAR

YEAR

YEAR

YEAR

YEAR

Laughter reflects a joyful heart! Who doesn't
like to hang with joyful, uplifting people?

November 27

YEAR

YEAR

YEAR

YEAR

YEAR

I choose to love others for who they are, not for what they
do or don't do. Lord, help me remember that the next
time I encounter my overflowing trash can.

November 28

YEAR

YEAR

YEAR

YEAR

YEAR

*Trust in the LORD with all your heart; do not depend
on your own understanding. Seek his will in all you do,
and he will show you which path to take.*
PROVERBS 3:5–6 NLT

YEAR

YEAR

YEAR

YEAR

YEAR

Trust: such an intimate form of faith. . . . Trust should cling to us like a second skin. . . . Thankfully, Papa God knows that it's a learning process for all of us. He's patiently waiting for our level of reliance to catch up and override our not-so-common sense as we take the plunge into trust.

November 30

YEAR

YEAR

YEAR

YEAR

YEAR

Don't be a wimp! Be a warrior!
Why settle for Olive Oyl when you could be Xena?

December 1

YEAR

YEAR

YEAR

YEAR

YEAR

Time to LOL!
God, Godiva, and girlfriends—what more do we need?

December 2

The LORD is good; His lovingkindness is everlasting.
PSALM 100:5 NASB

December 3

If God is in control, closed doors aren't accidental.
They're supposed to be closed. They're not an oversight
that slid by when God sneezed. They're part of the plan.

December 4

YEAR

YEAR

YEAR

YEAR

YEAR

Jesus, regardless of my appearance,
make me altogether lovely. . .like You.

December 5

YEAR

YEAR

YEAR

YEAR

YEAR

We can't change every situation, but through the Lord's power we can choose our responses to them. And that makes the difference between victory and defeat.

December 6

When you cross deep rivers, I will be with you, and you won't drown.
When you walk through fire, you won't be burned or scorched by the flames.
ISAIAH 43:2 CEV

December 7

YEAR

YEAR

YEAR

YEAR

YEAR

Power nap. Oooh, don't those two words send a tingle of anticipation down your spine? The pause that refreshes. Personal mini-vacation. Regrouping. Checking the eyelids for leaks. Stress-unloading. Closing up shop. Catching our breath. . . Whatever you call it, women need it.

December 8

YEAR

YEAR

YEAR

YEAR

YEAR

Just because I lose from time to time doesn't make me a *loser*.
A Christlike attitude and demonstrating God's grace under
fire determines who is a *winner*, not the score of a game.

December 9

YEAR
_____

YEAR
_____

YEAR
_____

YEAR
_____

YEAR
_____

Difficult people are often in our lives for unseen purposes. God's purposes.
Perhaps to stretch us, grow us, or sand down our sharp edges by their
friction. Remember, even nutty lumps in the batter add flavor!

December 10

I am surrounded by trouble, but you protect me. . . .
With your own powerful arm you keep me safe.
PSALM 138:7 CEV

December 11

YEAR

YEAR

YEAR

YEAR

YEAR

Prayer is about understanding what Papa God wants for us.

December 12

Our heavenly Father is our true BFFL He loves to hear our
twitter prayers—those little snippets we can shoot out at any time,
day or night, to keep us in constant communication.

December 13

YEAR

YEAR

YEAR

YEAR

YEAR

In the body of Christ, if we're hands, we wish we were feet;
if we're noses, we'd rather be eyes. Sometimes we feel like bunions.
But God views us as equally important. Even us toenails.

December 14

YEAR

YEAR

YEAR

YEAR

YEAR

The Lord will hold your hand,
and if you stumble, you still won't fall.
Psalm 37:24 CEV

December 15

When we're down in the dully-funks, the best way out of the
pit is to pile one kind deed on top of another and start climbing.

December 16

It's incredible how much difference a little optimism makes in reducing everyday stress. Everything looks surprisingly brighter, warmer, and more hopeful.

December 17

YEAR

YEAR

YEAR

YEAR

YEAR

I am merely a rosebud; Papa God is the Master Gardener. It's only because of His water, fertilizer, and loving care that I bloom and grow.

December 18

The Lord is good, a strong refuge when trouble comes.
He is close to those who trust in him.
NAHUM 1:7 NLT

December 19

Lord of all possibilities, fill me with dreams.
Big dreams. Your dreams for me.

December 20

YEAR

YEAR

YEAR

YEAR

YEAR

Didn't Jesus rebuke Martha for her preoccupation
as a human *do*-ing rather than a human *be*-ing?

December 21

YEAR

YEAR

YEAR

YEAR

Master Encourager, help me light up someone's life today—
to kindle their candle, not blow it out.

December 22

*Our LORD, we belong to you. We tell you
what worries us, and you won't let us fall.*
PSALM 55:22 CEV

December 23

Only God can turn us downside up!

December 24

YEAR

....

....

....

....

YEAR

....

....

....

....

YEAR

....

....

....

....

YEAR

....

....

....

....

YEAR

....

....

....

....

Creator of patience, fill my dry tank. Remind me when
I get frustrated that it's me who has the problem.

December 25

Papa God's cup of forgiveness is bottomless.

December 26

YEAR

YEAR

YEAR

YEAR

YEAR

Here on earth you will have many trials and sorrows.
But take heart, because I have overcome the world.
JOHN 16:33 NLT

December 27

YEAR

YEAR

YEAR

YEAR

YEAR

Sometimes when we feel least like doing something,
it's the very thing we need to do most.

December 28

YEAR

YEAR

YEAR

YEAR

YEAR

Think about it: What were your top three worries this time last year?
You're above average if you can remember more than one.
What does that tell you about the transient nature of worrying?

December 29

YEAR

YEAR

YEAR

YEAR

YEAR

Think about two areas of your life in which God has blessed you "far more abundantly beyond" your expectations. As we tread water in the stress-pool of life, we may not always *feel* blessed, but we definitely *are* blessed. Thank Him for His loving-kindness and provision.

December 30

God is a safe place to hide, ready to help when we need him. We stand fearless at the cliff-edge of doom, courageous in seastorm and earthquake, before the rush and roar of oceans, the tremors that shift mountains.
PSALM 46:1 MSG

December 31

YEAR ☐

....
....
....
....
....
....

YEAR ☐

....
....
....
....
....
....

YEAR ☐

....
....
....
....
....
....

YEAR ☐

....
....
....
....
....
....

YEAR ☐

....
....
....
....

Peace is acquired by intentionally handing our heavenly Father our daily
annoyances, dilemmas, and burdens one by one, minute by minute.
By giving up the steering wheel. . . . By making the choice to relax
in the backseat, enjoy the journey, and let Papa drive.

Enjoy these bonus readings from
Debora M. Coty's popular
Too Blessed to be Stressed!

Available wherever books are sold.

Lost and Found

—FAITH—

"If you had faith even as small as a mustard seed, you could say to this mountain, 'Move from here to there,' and it would move. Nothing would be impossible."

MATTHEW 17:20 NLT

I pull into my garage and pop open the trunk. My arms, already overflowing with bags from the front seat, threaten to give way as I combine as many items as possible with the groceries in back and haul them inside, trip after trip.

After slamming the trunk, I reach through the front passenger window for my purse, which lives on the little table thingie between the seats. It's not there.

This is not terribly alarming because my Big Bertha pocketbook has been known to, under the gravitational effects of inertia, launch from its little vehicular home like a guided missile when my brakes are forcefully engaged. Which is often.

Nope, it's not on the floorboards either.

Well, sometimes said purse plays roller derby, depending upon which direction my car was turning when the inertia took effect. So with much grunting and groaning, I grope beneath the seats and then along their sides. I unearth three pens; two fossilized apple cores; a stiff, blackened banana peel (so *that's* why I have a craving for banana bread every time I drive!); a dog-eared bookmark; $1.37 in change; the grocery list I lost three months ago; a package of dried-out hand wipes; a crusty fork; an almost-empty yogurt cup; and a tube of mascara. But no purse. I scan the underbellies of the backseats (my reverse driving has occasionally been compared to a bat flying out of somewhere exceptionally hot), but no sign of my purse.

Okay, now I'm starting to freak.

Lost my pocketbook? Oh, no, no, no! I can't lose that—*everything* is in there! My driver's license, credit cards, checkbook, insurance cards, receipts for all the clothes I need to return, my reading glasses, enough food to live for a month on a desert island, and most importantly, the last cherished square of that amazing German chocolate bar I bought on vacation last year.

It couldn't possibly all be gone! Tell me it ain't so!

I envision myself setting my handbag on top of my car to unlock my door and forgetting it's there and driving off. *Gulp.* I actually did that once with my CD case. Can you say crunchy vinyl? The innards of my purse could be strung out anywhere in the five miles between the grocery store and home. Haystack. Needles. *No!*

My overactive imagination kicks in and I picture a juvenile delinquent bicycle gang gathering my personal belongings like an Easter egg hunt and purchasing fourteen crates of Laffy Taffy with my credit cards. My angst transitions into rage when the nose-ringed, goth-haired punk in my mind smirks as he slides the last bite of my German chocolate bar onto his bolted tongue.

With heart racing, I storm into the kitchen to call the police. Forgetting the grocery bags lined up just inside the door, I trip and sprawl belly first on the tile floor, surrounded by scattering grapes, rolling cantaloupes, canned beans, and. . .my goodness, what is that? Lo and behold, it's my upended purse, liberated from the grocery bag I'd apparently stuffed it in when my memory was hibernating.

Whew! What relief! The knots in my stomach begin to uncoil. The banjo strings that were my neck cords relax. My purse was lost and now it's found. I was blind but now I see.

Life is so like that. We search everywhere for answers and get uptight and stressed out when the source of knowledge is in our possession the whole time. It's called the Bible.

During my two-year depression following six heart-wrenching

miscarriages, I searched for answers: Why? How could a loving God allow this to happen when we'd prayed and earnestly sought His guidance before each and every pregnancy? Had He abandoned me? It certainly felt like it. Or was He never really there to begin with?

Hard questions. Questions that either shape or shatter our faith. The kind each of us face when we're beaten down by devastating loss. When we can't pray and feel utterly hopeless. Lost without a map.

For a solid year I found no answers. Trite, canned platitudes from well-meaning people did nothing but infuriate me: "It's God's will—just accept it." "Look for the good in every situation." "If you had enough faith, you wouldn't find this so difficult."

Well, apparently I *didn't* have enough faith. Even after living as a Christ-follower for twenty-five years, I wasn't sure I had any faith at all. The hollowness in my soul threatened to devour me whole. Spiritual insecurity added more stress to my already overwhelmed existence.

In unadorned desperation, I turned to my Bible. The only place I *hadn't* looked.

I began reading the psalms, identifying with David as he bared his wounded heart. I found solace in the scream-at-God verses, like: "I dissolve my couch with my tears" (6:6 NASB); "I am poured out like water. . .my heart is like wax. . .melted within me" (22:14 NASB); "My sorrow is continually before me" (38:17 NASB); "Why do You hide Your face and forget our affliction and oppression?" (44:24 NASB); "My heart is in anguish within me" (55:4 NASB); "I looked for sympathy, but there was none, and for comforters, but I found none" (69:20 NASB); "Why do you withdraw Your hand?" (74:11 NASB); "I am so troubled that I cannot speak" (77:4 NASB); "You have taken me up and thrown me aside" (102:10 NIV); "Bring my soul out of prison" (142:7 NASB); and "My spirit is overwhelmed" (143:4 NASB).

David's cries of despair became my prayers—the only communication with God I could muster. But they cracked open the door. Gradually, over many months, the rock that was my heart began to crack from the inside out. God blessed my reluctant obedience in seeking nourishment—no, life itself—from His Word.

Sometimes when we feel least like doing something, it's the very thing we need to do most. I kept reading every day out of sheer obedience and progressed to the help-me-trust-again psalm verses like: "The LORD is my shepherd, I shall not want. . . . Your rod and Your staff, they comfort me" (23:1, 4 NASB); "Turn to me and be gracious to me, for I am lonely and afflicted" (25:16 NASB); "Weeping may last for the night, but a shout of joy comes in the morning" (30:5 NASB); "Be gracious to me, O LORD, for I am in distress" (31:9 NASB); "I sought the LORD and He answered me and delivered me from all my fears" (34:4 NASB); "Rest in the LORD and wait patiently for Him" (37:7 NASB); "Why, my soul, are you downcast? . . . Put your hope in God, for I will yet praise him" (42:11 NIV); and "Cease striving and know that I am God" (46:10 NASB). Other psalms offering hope and healing are 56, 63, 119, 121, and 139.

Within those pages I'd stumbled upon a map, but I didn't realize I was actually clawing my way out of my lost, dark cavern until I saw light peeking over the rim.

God's Word seeped into my parched spirit like a healing spring of water. By praying through the psalms, something unexplainable changed inside me. My circumstances hadn't been altered. I still had no sweet baby to cuddle. But somehow a seed of trust in the Great Healer had taken root and bloomed inside me like a fragrant flower.

I was once again able to praise my heavenly Father through psalms like: "You, LORD, are. . .the One who lifts my head high" (3:3 NIV); "In peace I will both lie down and sleep" (4:8 NASB); "He does not forget the cry of the afflicted" (9:12 NASB); "I love you, O LORD, my strength" (18:1 NASB); "We will sing for joy over your victory" (20:5 NASB); "My flesh and my heart may fail, but God is the strength of my heart and my portion forever" (73:26 NASB); "How blessed is the man who trusts in You" (84:12 NASB); "He will cover you with his feathers, and under his wings you will find refuge" (91:4 NIV); "Great is the LORD and greatly to be praised" (96:4 NASB); "The LORD is good; His lovingkindness is everlasting and His faithfulness to all generations" (100:5 NASB); "I love the LORD, for he heard my voice; he heard my cry for mercy" (116:1 NIV); and "He heals the brokenhearted and binds up their wounds" (147:3 NIV).

After this searching process—and it is a process, not a sudden discovery—my relationship with my loving heavenly Father was fully and gloriously restored. Supernatural peace soothed my tattered nerves.

Healing takes effort on our part; we can't just sit like a limp, wounded lump and wait for it to hit us. We have to dig deep for the courage to reach out for help from the very source of our pain. Or so we perceive. But then by God's grace we *will* find what was really never lost.

On a lighter note, I believe misplacing things like my purse is hormonal. Of course, I blame everything on hormones. Just haven't figured out why the fewer hormones I have as I age, the more things I lose. I have noticed, though, that the things I've found that once were lost become oh, so much more precious.

Like faith. And German chocolate. *Mmm.*

Faith can move mountains, but don't be surprised if God hands you a shovel.

UNKNOWN

LET'S DECOM-STRESS

1. Have you ever gone through a time when you felt like you had lost your faith? How did you find it again?

2. When you feel wounded, where do you turn for healing?

3. Remember this chapter, dear sister, and the next time you feel that your pain is estranging you from God, begin praying through the psalms I've outlined. You will not believe how lifting God's Word up to Him in prayer will miraculously mend your broken heart. I'm praying for you.

All Stressed Up and Nowhere to Break Down
—Coping with Loss—

*He has never let you down, never looked the
other way when you were being kicked around.
He has never wandered off to do his own thing;
he has been right there, listening.*
PSALM 22:24 MSG

❧ The voice on the phone fades into oblivion as the forgotten
instrument slowly drops from your quivering hand at 3 a.m.

❧ The slamming door sets your world spinning as if gravity
has abandoned you, too.

❧ You hear but can't grasp the doctor's grave words as they
tumble deep into a dark, cavernous pit inside your gut.

Bad news. Sudden devastating loss. Unexpected catastrophe.

It's true: We're all just one phone call from our knees. Shattering
loss happens to all of us at some time in our lives. How do we deal
with it? How do we get past the spiritual, physical, and emotional
paralysis that often accompanies shock? How do we avoid complete
and utter wipeout?

Please allow me to share successful coping skills from several
godly women who have suffered life-altering losses.

After twenty-eight years of marriage, my friend Lauren's husband
presented her with a pronouncement out of the blue: "I'm leaving
you."

For years Lauren had struggled to hold down two jobs while

simultaneously completing college courses to provide for their family of six when John could no longer work or drive due to a debilitating neurological disease. She chauffeured John to endless medical appointments and devotedly cared for her husband's special needs. Lauren was completely blindsided when John decided that she was somehow holding him back from getting well.

No one knows more than my friend Esther about desperately grasping the hope offered in 1 Corinthians 10:13 (MSG): "God will never let you down; he'll never let you be pushed past your limit; he'll always be there to help you come through it."

Esther's two-year-old son, Adam, was diagnosed with a rare, aggressive form of cancer. For two agonizing years, Esther endured with her baby through chemotherapy, hospitalization for amputation of his arm, and futile attempts to assuage his pain before God took Adam home on Valentine's Day. Heartsick, Esther sank into despair and depression to the point of attempting to take her own life.

"When I look back, I see that even as I struggled, Jesus was the one that carried me and gave me life for here and hereafter," Esther says today. "Jesus is the *only* way of escape in terrible situations. As believers, we truly can find strength to overcome and endure trials through the love of Christ."

In times of acute distress, the wheels of everyday life may grind to a screeching, jarring halt. We feel helpless, clueless as to how to lubricate those rusty cogs to set the wheels back in motion and move forward. Based on the experiences of Lauren, Esther, and others who have suffered loss, perhaps those wheels just need a little G-R-E-A-S-E:

G: Grieve. It's okay, dear sister. Mourning is part of the healing process. The pain is deep. Allow yourself to *feel* your loss. The death of a dream can feel as real as the death of a loved one. Denying or ignoring reality only postpones the inevitable. Keep your eyes on Jesus through the grief process; remember, it's His power, His presence that ultimately heals. God really does do broken-heart surgery.

R: Release. Pour out your feelings to Papa God. He understands loss—His beloved Son was ruthlessly beaten and killed. Go ahead, pound on His chest. Scream. Sob. He's a very *big* God. He can take it.

Be assured that crying jags and energy lags are perfectly normal post-crisis release mechanisms. You're in mourning and your body is reacting to your spirit trying to reconcile your loss. You often feel as if you're running on empty and you haven't a clue where or how to refill your tank. Papa God gets it. He owns the pump.

Special note: It's important to set time parameters so healthy release doesn't continue indefinitely and become an unhealthy quagmire of unproductive anger.

E: Establish support. Find a source of regular, ongoing emotional support like a group of like-minded, caring women or a trusted friend. People who are safe and understand your vulnerability. Accept their strength to bolster you when yours is gone.

A: Act. Get off that couch, girl. Move your bones. Put one foot in front of the other. Now do it again. Go out. Keep breathing. Keep living. Don't allow yourself to fold up and wither away. You may not *feel* like doing squat, but long-term happiness trumps short-term sacrifice. Remember, healing is a dollar off coupon, not a blow-out sale. It's an incremental process. Step by tiny step, just keep moving in the right direction and eventually you'll get there. You will!

S: Seek godly counsel. Schedule regular sessions with a *Christian* counselor. It's important to get a scriptural perspective during your healing process. You wouldn't ask your hair stylist to fix your car, would you? Of course not—it's not her area of expertise. Your soul is infinitely more important than your carburetor. Seek guidance from a trained representative of your Creator who is entrenched in godly values and spiritual principles.

E: Exercise. Okay, now it's time for some tough self-discipline. Set a specific regular routine, not just vague promises like "I'll climb more steps," but something measurable like, "Four flights of stairs each day" or "I'll bike to the park three times every week." Then hold yourself accountable by a checklist. Walk, run, ski, spin, work out, join the roller derby—whatever waxes your eyebrows, but make it a priority. No weasel words: "*Maybe* I'll go," "*Probably* tomorrow," "*If* it doesn't rain and Jupiter aligns with Mars." Listen, you can't control disasters, but you *can* control whether or not you provide your body the physical outlet it needs to keep your natural chemicals and healing fluids pumping. Do this for *you.*

I believe it's fair to say that 95 percent of us question God's love for us and even His very existence when tragedy strikes. And in our fallen world, it *will* strike everyone at one time or another. My husband Chuck and I both went through our own barren desert times in our faith after six heart-wrenching miscarriages. We estranged ourselves from the Lord and wanted nothing more to do with a god who we felt didn't care about us. My desert lasted three lonely years—bad enough—but Chuck's dragged on for a decade.

In the immediate throes of our loss, God seemed cruel and heartless. We felt abandoned and lost, but in retrospect, like Esther, we now see that God was still there all along. Not cruel, not heartless, just silently shining a flashlight of hope and waiting patiently for our self-imposed spiritual cataracts to slough off so we could see His presence.

One of my favorite scriptures of comfort became Psalm 22:24 (look back at the beginning of this chapter). I came to understand that God is not our afflict*or*; no, He's the helper of the afflict*ed*. That's you and me. He's not the enemy; He's on our team. A huge difference to a healing heart!

Another coping truth recently came to me in my girlcave. (Some call it a kitchen.)

Have you ever baked homemade bread? Nothing smells better

this side of heaven! Well, the way I see it, healing is like bread yeast—the dough has to be pulled, stretched, and beat upon to work the yeast throughout, but it finally permeates every inch. Over time, that very yeast enables the bread to rise and become what it was meant to be. If the yeast doesn't pervade the dough, or if the loaf doesn't spend enough time in the oven, the bread will never be completed. It will always remain useless, gloppy, inedible dough. Heat is necessary for its transformation and perfection.

So the next time you feel like yelling, "Stick a toothpick in me; I'm done!" remember that although our oven days are difficult—often painful—those are the times we grow and mature in our faith.

I have learned that pain has purpose, which, at the peak of excruciating discomfort, brings me little consolation. Hindsight, though, has often proven pain's value. In fact, I have found pain to be one of life's most effective teachers.

PATSY CLAIRMONT

LET'S DECOM-STRESS

1. Describe a recent time when you faced devastating, unexpected loss. How did you deal with it? Are you still dealing with it?

2. Which of the GREASE elements did you implement? Which did you not use? Do you see a need to implement them now?

3. Read Psalm 4 (it's short). How, like David, can we find peace in our distress? What does it mean to be "set apart" (verse 3)?

About the Author

Debora M. Coty is a popular humorist, speaker, and award-winning author of numerous inspirational books, including the bestselling *Too Blessed to be Stressed* line. Deb considers herself a tennis junkie and choco-athlete (meaning she exercises just so she can eat more chocolate). A retired piano teacher and orthopedic occupational therapist, Debora currently lives, loves, and laughs in central Florida with her husband Chuck and three adorable grandbuddies who live next door. Visit with Deb at www.DeboraCoty. com and follow her antics on Facebook, Twitter, and Instagram. Connect with her via her "Life in the Crazy Lane" blog at www.DeboraCoty.blogspot.com.

More Titles to Keep Your Life De-Stressed!

Too Blessed to Be Stressed: 3-Minute Devotions for Women

Women will find the spiritual pick-me-up they desire in *Too Blessed to Be Stressed: 3-Minute Devotions for Women*. 180 uplifting readings from bestselling author Debora M. Coty pack a powerful dose of comfort, encouragement, humor, and inspiration into just-right-sized readings for women on the go.
Paperback / 978-1-63409-569-3 / $4.99

Too Blessed to Be Stressed Cookbook

The *Too Blessed to Be Stressed Cookbook* offers 100-plus recipes that can be prepared in 20 minutes or less, along with fabulous tips and suggestions as well as funny foodie quotes, scripture selections, humorous stories of cooking misadventures, and more. Recipes are arranged into 4 categories—Heart-Healthy, Soul-Fed, Time-Wise, and Company-Happy—and are accompanied by appealing full-color photographs.
Hardback / 978-1-63409-322-4 / $16.99

Too Blessed to Be Stressed Coloring Book

Color your way to calm with the delightful *Too Blessed to be Stressed Coloring Book* from popular inspirational humorist, Debora M. Coty. Forty-five unique images on quality stock will comfort and inspire through beautiful design, refreshing thoughts, and scripture selections. The backs of each generous 8x10 coloring page are left blank—perfect for coloring with crayons, colored pencils, and markers.
Paperback / 978-1-63409-969-1 / $9.99